A book of the heart and soul of the one that has communion with powerful words.

— *Elder Randy Simmons*

The content within the pages of this book is of such high value... not just from the perspective of brain stimulation, but from the perspective of how life works... The writings of these poems can apply to; LIFE itself, Business Principles, Leadership Mindset, & Personal Development...All things needed to succeed. Well done!

— *Steve Carter*
Entrepreneur, Investor, Professional Network Marketer,
Personal Development & Success Coach

The Objective Scholar is an adventurous journey into our minds, hearts and dreams. Troy's words will guide you into deep thoughts, feelings and imaginational visions. I highly recommend this journey!

— *Brad Richard*
Certified Master Life Coach, Author, Speaker & Podcast Host

Refreshing, thought-provoking and inspirational, hope there is more to come!

— *Ken Walters*
Ken Walters Promotions & Products

Praise for *The Objective Scholar*

For us, Troy is the Super Hero of an endangered species: poets. With his second book he puts on his bright cape again, only this time to arm women from all backgrounds with powerful words of wisdom.

> — *Mario P. Cloutier*
> *Relationship Coach, Author, Huffington Post Blogger*

Overall, Troy Legette's collection of poems in this book are absolutely self-liberating. Not only do they showcase his gifted artistry, the poems clearly invite the reader to enter a poetic, heartfelt place of inner-healing and self-transformation.

> — *Professor Gary L. Lemons, Ph.D.*
> *Department of English, University of South Florida*

Troy Legette's most recent collection, *The Objective Scholar,* is a true representation of his dedication to the craft of poetry. If poetry is a poet's contribution to the world, this book is his offering to the ages. Read and remember. Read and remember.

> — *Hiram Sims*
> *Founder, Community Literature Initiative (CLI)*

The collection is organized thematically, each section representing a different facet of life's intricate tapestry. Legette delves into the universal themes that connect us all, from love and loss to self-discovery and resilience. His ability to weave and express complex emotions with simplicity and grace is a testament to his indigenous experience and intellectual mastery of language.

> — *Professor Dr. LaMont Flanagan*
> *University of Maryland, Global Campus*

Troy Legette explores self-awareness in this collection. His poetic practice is clearly a means to self-improvement, which inspires his readers to travel down this road with him to a higher plane of growth.

> — *Professor Lisa Montagne, Ed.D.*
> *Community Literature Initiative (CLI)*

This content provides a valuable perspective on the importance of earning money through meaningful and ethical means, emphasizing gratitude for life's intangible treasures. The poetic expression adds depth to the message, urging readers to prioritize personal fulfillment over mere financial gains. A thoughtful reminder to appreciate life's lessons and the unique journey each individual undertakes.

> — *Ronni A Oats Jr.*
> *Agency Owner, Brightway Insurance - The Oats Agency.*

I met Troy R. Legette a few years ago at a signing of his first book, *Social Climax*. I find Troy to be extremely passionate about his work. Reading his poems I see his wonderful soul and spirit. His new book, *The Objective Scholar – Poetic Wordplay*, is a collection I found refreshing and insightful. Written with the heart of a true poet, you will not be disappointed. Both works of art, they are compelling and honest.

> — *Marla Shaw O'Neill*
> *Author of* Sing Sarah Sing, Pray Pearl, Pray *and* God's Heartbeat Ba-bump

THE OBJECTIVE SCHOLAR

THE OBJECTIVE SCHOLAR
POETIC WORDPLAY

Troy R. Legette

The Objective Scholar: Poetic Wordplay
© 2024 Troy R. Legette
ISBN: 979-8-9898262-0-9 (paperback)
ISBN: 979-8-9898262-1-6 (hardback)
ISBN: 979-8-9898262-2-3 (ebook)
ISBN: 979-8-9898262-3-0 (audio book)
Library of Congress Control Number: 2024905523

First Edition, 2024

Published in Tampa, Florida
Printed in the United States of America

Edited by Meagan Duncan
Cover Design by Adam Martinez
Layout Design by Kean Towle & Emily Anne Evans

*M*uch love and respect to all readers:

May this book find you in the best receptive moment of your life. I ask you to sincerely understand nothing is meant to degrade, disrespect, or make you feel offended in any way. The intention is to uplift, motivate, encourage, and inspire.

This book is a tool for everyone who supported me throughout my years. The family and friends who always showed me love and support. The many mentors taking responsibility for my development as a civilized human being. The teachers that are educating me. The prisoners that shared their eyeglasses to help me see a nonfiction reality. My birthplace in New Jersey. My current residence in Florida.

This is a book that has been in the making since 2015 following my first self-published poetry collection titled *Social Climax*.

Contents

Impartial Portrait

Dinkum Proclivity

Communal Sentiment

Distinctive Subjection

Abstract Dopamine

Lyrics (Bonus Section)

Word Search: Find the *styles of poetry* listed to the right.

```
E  B  G  K  W  M  L  Y  D  O  M  L  F
X  L  A  U  A  V  A  Z  X  D  T  C  R
D  Y  L  I  Y  S  O  L  K  U  W  Q  E
M  R  P  E  S  B  J  U  J  T  V  X  E
Q  I  T  E  N  P  M  B  C  E  O  A  V
S  C  X  M  C  A  K  J  W  N  B  L  E
R  B  W  I  Q  C  L  I  D  N  S  Q  R
L  K  D  J  H  P  Q  L  V  O  U  L  S
G  M  I  W  L  O  Z  O  I  S  M  D  E
I  W  T  P  A  W  V  R  Z  V  R  B  Z
J  A  Y  D  L  P  M  Z  B  N  K  V  U
C  R  F  B  R  A  W  N  H  B  A  K  W
Q  U  M  A  Q  L  Z  C  O  F  I  O  M
O  S  V  L  N  X  S  A  I  A  H  M  Z
T  E  R  L  P  M  S  E  H  S  P  C  R
U  A  P  A  Q  U  N  X  L  G  Z  A  L
Q  C  G  D  T  A  S  Q  K  D  V  C  S
J  Z  D  T  H  E  B  W  N  Q  J  L  F
D  A  K  J  S  T  I  Z  X  A  H  M  Q
O  Z  B  T  A  M  W  B  O  Q  S  D  A
Q  S  I  C  I  T  S  A  R  H  P  K  E
M  N  F  R  Y  G  V  X  L  P  I  Y  K
A  X  T  K  P  A  N  T  O  U  M  O  Q
```

Preface

*D*uring the many years since my first book of poetry, *Social Climax*, I've been in deep thought deciphering the best way to deliver to you a part of me you can embrace. I figured clarity, if it isn't boring, would suit and fulfill the purpose.

In this book, I wrote with the intention of experiencing various styles of poetry within the literary industry. Some of the styles are:

• *Haiku*	• *Lyric*	• *Sestina*
• *Ballad*	• *Caesura*	• *Pantoum*
• *Essay*	• *Sonnet*	• *Villanelle*
• *Ekphrastic*	• *Ghazal*	• *Free Verse*

A place where we follow and break the rules a bit to create enjoyment. Topics are more relatable to the everyday person in some kind of way.

THE OBJECTIVE SCHOLAR
POETIC WORDPLAY

Moralistic Scope

Independent Thinker

*N*othing in the world compares to accurate decision-making:
partaking in the lead...yes! Determined by no other,
minus concrete and ferocious arrogance
for the results to replicate at will.

Tunnel vision cold as winter snowflaking,
unaware of thoughts, the mind discovers
character floating in the name of eloquence
for the depth is calm still.

Different in a sense of hot water shaking,
each point seems like twin brothers,
game plan intimate, and tasteful romance
for the delivery mimic skill.

Driven by heat, impulse baking
alone consistently without useless smother
unidentified within the eyes at first glance
for levels rest on top of a hill.

Learning

*E*very day I'm learning...
By keeping an open mind about the
situation, even though I have to humble
myself enough
to accept the fact that I can't fault myself,
for the things I do not know.

The definition of *"effort"* in my own words is when one:
- Take a step forward.
- Engages in an activity on one's own accord.
- Honestly attempts at doing something.

Every day I'm learning...
By keeping an open mind about the
situation, even though I have to humble
myself enough
to accept the fact that I can't fault myself,
for the things I do not know.

The definition of *"priorities"* in my own words is:
- Placing focus on what matters most.
- The most valued approached in chronological order.
- When human action towards an makes sense.

Every day I'm learning...
By keeping an open mind about the
situation, even though I have to humble
myself enough
to accept the fact that I can't fault myself,
for the things I do not know.

The definition of *"maturity"* in my own words is:
- The process of internal development.
- Achieving in a way that each bullet point equals success.
- When a seed is planted and the flower blooms.

Every day I'm learning...
By keeping an open mind about the
situation, even though I have to humble
myself enough
to accept the fact that I can't fault myself,
for the things I do not know.

The Reason

Smart people are the reason,

> The world has evolved into a spiral.
> There is a misinterpretation of inspiration and jealousy.

Smart people are the reason,

> For some, it is natural, and for others, a challenge.
> For thinking that hurting a character is lazily described.

Faux Invisible

Be careful! There's an eye connected to an evil mind
actively at work. Its sole purpose is to eradicate your
name and character. Therefore, it's imperative that you
love yourself in a way you're protected.

Our highest involvement can lead to territory
displaying misconceptions about true intentions.
For example, when we drive cars on the road and are
conscious of the other drivers doing the same.

Tensely anticipating reactions to what may cause an accident.
Life encounters require the same frame of mind. Whether
you're in the cities of New Jersey or the country southern
congenial towns in lovely Florida.

Paying attention to people, places, and things on a daily basis
is paramount to reading and writing. There are many distractions
along with hate and crave for your downfall. And the funny thing
is it has an invisible presence.

Be careful! There's an eye connected to an evil mind
actively at work. Its sole purpose is to eradicate your
name and character. Therefore, it's imperative that you
love yourself in a way you're protected.

All Money

All money is not good money especially if it's not earned
in a way where regret or disappointment taunts you.

Believe it or not, there's a higher top
living thankful for what you got,
something more than a lot:

> • A mind, a heart, and two feet to walk
> • A mouth to talk, plus life lessons taught
> • All at an expense not paid nor bought

All money is not good money especially if it's not earned
in a way that regrets or disappointment taunts you.

Enjoy what you do, the only judge is you.
Always be true, each day new,
many skies are blue, and some days are gray too.

Spice up the menu. Always continue!
Each shoe worn is its individual,
highly intellectual molded by what you have been through.

All money is not good money especially if it's not earned
in a way that regrets or disappointment taunts you.

Looking for Information

Pay attention to the clever wordplay,
I call a foul use of psychology in a conversation –
they're just looking for information.

Accumulating components based around theory
or opinion to use uncontrollably and even flagrant.
So unclassy! That description fits perfectly.

In an attempt to present a misleading façade,
only to justify the reason why the unwanted
prying is so forceful.

Make Everything Count

Limits slow progress.
The determined focus forward,
the hesitant ebb.

Crafty by nature,
intelligence reflects tone.
Zipped within strong webs.

Designed from fine strands.
Collected to build sangfroid.
Illuminating!

Marriage is No Fairy Tale

*T*he talk of it all is so exciting!
In the beginning it appears easy.
Time passes, adopting life memories.
Tricked by thoughts of intimate rendezvous.
White picket fence is gray aluminum.
Morning breakfast ends after a few months.
The attraction fades once the pounds increase.
That personal space shrivels like raisins.
Love becomes based on financial status.
Mystery involves who's cooking tonight.
Lost urges of lust entertain white lies.
Trust begins ignoring honest intent.
Soft sexy tones turn into loud yelling.
Laundry days delayed foul odor smelling.

Now We Know

*I*t is your beauty they envy.
My gender is the opposite.
My gender is the reason.
Hate enacted a plot to create something similar.

I speak on behalf of all of you left vulnerable,
alone with an experience unfavorable.
An unfavorable feeling that violated your business.
Violated your freedom of happiness or preferential choice.

I'm a voice-speaker who understands such confusion.
A mistaken identity you now mirror.
A mirror reflected as an image disrespected.
By chivalry preying on the young of innocence.

Stimulating psychological damage unforgiven.
An internal prison marinating revenge,
now intimate with the thought.

Practicing a relationship is habitual.
Normal as days your existence surrendered.
Feeling trapped by your gender.
A gender that portrays my same gender.

Taken forcefully using fear.
The picture is clear and now protected by law.
A law that satisfied secret infliction,
co-signing biblical information — the last days.

Formulating inquisitive assumptions presumed relevant,
as youth succumb to acceptance.
Succumb to the influence of not knowing.
Ignorant to natural reproduction and its importance.

Mother's Day

*L*oving and Special!
Number one parent teacher,
protective leader.

Guidance director,
deserved appreciation.
Ultimate woman!

Respectfully, thanks!
Nurturer and provider!
Above all others!

The Real World

$\mathcal{Y}$ou see the real world
It tells us no lies!
I mean, it's so honest.
When you listen and get it,
you understand that what you have been doing is
the reason you are feeling the way you do.

In the present moment,
the list includes:
- Self-analysis
- Physical space and presence
- Peace of mind
- Communication
- Respect
- Relationships
- Coexistence
- Habits
- Awareness
- Love
- Goals
- Culture
- Facts and truth

You see the real world
It tells us no lies!
I mean, it's so honest.
When you listen and get it,
you understand that what you have been doing is
the reason you are feeling the way you do.

Labor Day

*F*irst Monday honored;
US public holiday,
Labor Day movement.

- Organized parade
- The Central Labor Union
- In New York City

Supporting workers;
Street parades and barbecues.
Celebrating thanks!

Reserved Esse

𝑀oments of disparity are often taken for granted.
　Some things in life are uncontrollable, Hurricane Ian's the proof,
　fierce winds at approximately 150 mph pulling shingles off roofs.
A category 4 along the Southern Florida coasts caused major damage.

Ocean top tumbles terrain and floods.
　Evacuation measures that's needed are most necessary.
　Uninvited wildlife floating strange and out of the ordinary,
disturbing news regarding the life of each loved one.

This State of Emergency calls for immediate response orders
　from Federal disaster aid to the rescue from various states.
　Wishing that people can escape and be safe.
Power shortages needed assistance: generators, food, shelter, water.

Aftermath effects from the destruction and grief.
　Voluntary support extending helping hands.
　Prayers from those at a distant and even faraway lands,
money for a greater cause, thanks to Wells Fargo's 1 million relief!

Qualified

So, finally, I graduated with my Bachelor's Degree each day counting. Now, I am ready to exercise my skills and gain more experience without a doubt. Besides, I know I qualify according to the newspaper classified section, spirit bouncing. Wait for a second, what happened now they want a Master's Degree from me in accounting?

My current job does not pay me enough to cover all my bills. I have nothing to lose, so it's off to get enrolled for my Master's Degree at will. Three years later, I have another Degree under my belt, and yet still. I'm applying to better positions for better pay (pushing forward uphill).

A new day, I'm so excited and headed to my first interview. I arrived on time and performed like a superstar, sharply dressed. In front of the computer emailing my thank you, you would know I will get hired next. Only to be told I'm overqualified and they found a better candidate with a CPA who fits best.

My determination had me at another interview several days later just like magic. Continuously increasing my game plan as I approach using a strategic angle tactic. Every question answered with precise deliverance attracted. Only to be told I will contact you in a couple of days which turned into never contacted.

Picking my self-esteem up off the ground, I push forward steadily. My phone rings... Yes, the big one! Somebody decided to contact me for a position I won't avoid. All I heard when I answered was the sounds of a man's voice. I mean I could hardly understand anything that was said but a 3-month contract position choice.

Now, in my mind, I'm thinking this cannot be real. I've worked four contract positions and now somebody is calling about another one, what is the deal? So, in my slight voice, I kindly said, "Please, tell me more about the contract position, I got bills. The job I had previously ended right after finishing my Master's Degree gave me the chills."

Any income is better than being in an unemployed trap. So, I agreed to take the position and as soon as we hung up the phone, I'm contacted back. This time, it wasn't to offer me another job or confirm an interview, so that's that. It was to let me know that they needed someone with experience. I don't even have crap.

Forcing me to go back to the drawing board and upgrade the special game plan grid. Now, it has been approximately two years since I have been pursuing accounting positions. All of which I went to school for, got granted school loans, and worked low-paying part-time gigs. None of which are accounting. Yet, I still see positions in the newspaper classified section where I live.

Lil Boy Elroy

Lil Boy Elroy finds brilliance being uneducated
Figure life is better living by his own rules
Disrespectful to his parents
Chooses to drop out of school
He is so cool, people think he's a fool

Too young to get hired by an employer
Too smart to live in a safe home
Hustle to be his own supporter
Abandoned into the wilderness alone

Living on the edge approaching traps
Living on the edge taking risk
Living on the edge wearing different hats
Living on the edge hoping to get rich

Lil Boy Elroy finds brilliance being uneducated
Figure life is better living by his own rules
Disrespectful to his parents
Chooses to drop out of school
He is so cool, people think he's a fool

Finds a friend who moves him in
In hopes of a better life
Until his attitude causes arguments and leaves again
Back to roaming the wilderness, now that's twice

Striving to make ends meet turns to crime
Striving to make ends meet working as a thief
Striving to make ends meet continuously master telling lies
Striving to make ends meet lusting greed

Lil Boy Elroy finds brilliance being uneducated
Figure life is better living by his own rules
Disrespectful to his parents
Chooses to drop out of school
He is so cool, people think he's a fool

One day he met his match
Crossing a road, hit by a stray bullet
Laying in a puddle of blood—Karma's wrath
The violence of a trigger—no one knows who pulled it

Lying there nearly bleeding to death
Lying there in shock
Lying there needing EMS help
Lying there hoping the bleeding stop

Lil Boy Elroy finds brilliance being uneducated
Figure life is better living by his own rules
Disrespectful to his parents
Chooses to drop out of school
He is so cool, people think he's a fool

Ambulance breathing life's first beginnings
Hospitalized!
Frightened by trauma—world spinning
Frustrated and traumatized!

Trying hard to maintain the pain
Trying hard to not to cry
Trying hard to regain a conscious mind-frame
Trying hard to understand why

Lil Boy Elroy finds brilliance being uneducated
Figure life is better living by his own rules
Disrespectful to his parents
Chooses to drop out of school
He is so cool, people think he's a fool

New focus to rehabilitate
Heart grows a greater love
Stuck in a situation he can't escape
The funny things that life does

Crying from the immediate state of emergency
Crying from the chaos
Crying from the white T-Shirt colored burgundy
Crying from the site as others watch

Lil Boy Elroy finds brilliance being uneducated
Figure life is better living by his own rules
Disrespectful to his parents
Chooses to drop out of school
He is so cool, people think he's a fool

His mindset tends to think a bit different
Viewpoint on life changes
Read more to overcome his ignorance
Now he understands the value instead of living aimless

Beginning to accept reformation
Beginning to accept a voice in spirit
Beginning to accept a new and true confirmation
Beginning to accept every time he hears it

Lil Boy Elroy finds brilliance being uneducated
Figure life is better living by his own rules
Disrespectful to his parents
Chooses to drop out of school
He is so cool, people think he's a fool

He is so smooth, he makes friends with the nurses
Promised his family to do better
Asks God to help him comprehend Bible verses
Even wrote some childhood friends letters

Relying on a ton of external efforts and socialization
Relying on reliable support
Relying on confidence and determination
Relying on help from a higher force

Lil Boy Elroy finds brilliance being uneducated
Figure life is better living by his own rules
Disrespectful to his parents
Chooses to drop out of school
He is so cool, people think he's a fool

Realizing that he has no feeling on the left side of his body
Trusting the process and time to heal
The Doctor thinks it's permanent probably
He never imagined this situation could be real

Defying the odds by pushing forward
Defying the odds by thinking positive
Defying the odds by following what the Doctor ordered
Defying the odds by executing the main objectives

Let The Money Talk

You need to quit! Honestly, do you think it's a safe
or better place to host banknotes irresponsibly?
A region stitched to a pair of slacks,
sitting dormant?
The brightest mind is one,
that implements ways to let the money talk.

Let's see! We all have the ability to develop
talents attached to a specific and natural act of performance.
There are so many investors in the world.
It makes a lot of sense to become an investor of our own.

Not to mention reaping the benefits of higher education.
Some certifications and licenses assist with greatness.
Most choices and decisions come with no price.
Only one day, to allow the opportunity of creating our own.

Finally, there is always a real-life monopoly game going on:
Commercial or residential.
I'm the biggest fan when money lives as a verb.
Circulating sporadically!
Worldwide allows us to hold our own.

You need to quit! Honestly, do you think it's a safe
or better place to host banknotes irresponsibly?
A region stitched to a pair of slacks,
sitting dormant?
The brightest mind is one,
that implements ways to let the money talk.

Photo Credit: Troy LeGette

Valentine's Day

*C*omplimenting cards:
Love, roses, and heart moments,
intimate passion.

Ingenious Competence

It's

*I*t's an art created within.
I have no reason,
for such perfection.

It's an urge that developed.
I'm unable to stop.
It's continuous.

It's a love I never knew,
I will cherish it.
Now and Forever!

It's precise, wise words spoken.
Freedom of voicing,
all ears should listen.

Its thoughts are shared openly.
Everyone relates,
simple and complex.

It's an awesome life of breath,
inhale and exhale.
Eternal life's source.

Photography

$\mathcal{L}$ights, camera, action!
The perfect image captured,
forever lasting.

Some Meal

Okay, it's finally my turn to show off what I'm made of. You had
yours; now, it's mine. Alright, so before I begin, I will kindly
wipe the countertop with a warm wet rag. Then place
two cutting boards near the sink:
One for cutting up my veggies. I'm talking onions, garlic, broccoli, and
some potatoes. The other will be chicken breast which I will slice
neatly into tenders the size of fingers.
Hold up, let me run out to the car
to grab the two aluminum pans, I purchased from the Dollar Store.
Throwaways, always save time when cleaning the kitchen. Okay,
I'm back, now yesterday that delicious plate you made for me keep
my memory tingling.
Heck, it inspired me to wake up this beautiful and sunny
morning, and return the favor.
Now, I don't know whose recipe you stole... lol!
But I'm sure if it told anyone this little secret,
our nights alone eating dinner together
would end. I say that because the restaurant offers more delicacies.
Asking you to stand over someone else's stove
not to mention for someone else's business
would gladly entertain your time and I'd be pissed.
So, before I let that inconvenience happen in my life,
I will challenge myself to create something
similar that will have your taste buds dancing and grooving
as if you swallowed a pill called "Paula Abdul".
What? Why are you laughing at me? I'm serious!
My goal is to bake veggies soft enough that you barely have to bite
down with force...
Oh! And the chicken? No question, it will melt in your mouth like
hot chocolate bathing under the sun at Siesta Keys beach.

So, here goes nothing...
Finally, the table is set and everyone's plate
Is slowly elevating smoke
as if a vent breathing deeply and high above.
Adrenaline rushes pounding my chest.
Hold up! Is somebody knocking at the door?
Oh, my mind must be playing tricks on me again.
Pardon that minor interruption and back to business.
So, here goes nothing...
Here, taste this, come on into your mouth.
I'm so excited to know what you think.
Now, before I even ask if we can continue,
Your eyes look like a waterfall.
What's the matter?
Are you surprised?
Your boy can throw down, right?
Would you like a napkin?
That way, you can wipe your eyes,
Or a drink to clear your throat.
Wait for a minute baby;
Where are you going?
Oh! The bathroom,
It's cool!
I will wait here...

Puppy Love

$\mathcal{T}$ he minute I laid eyes on her, I was captured;
Captured by the innocence of infancy.
Laying there next to two others covered in fleas.
Fleas were attached to them like skin.
Without hesitation, I scooped them out of a box in the truck.
The truck was parked in the garage where I worked.
Drove them to my apartment to feed them;
Feed them puppy Blue Buffalo.
Purchased flea-fighting shampoo.
Shampoo used on them while bathing.
Removed every single flea from their bodies.
Their bodies are so fragile and delicate.
I call them the three musketeer puppies!
Puppies whose lives were saved from those viscous fleas.
The good heart came through.
Through at a time of need without a pause.

Reading

*N*ecessary tool!
Find it everywhere in life.
No way around it.

Unforgettable Liaison

You are!
Exposed emotions.
Now humor my efforts.
Make it last until fireworks burst.
Trust me!

Listen!
Words penetrate,
ringing eardrums softly.
Applied, tonic soothing teaspoons.
Freshly!

Heartbeats,
spill openly.
Traveling love transferred.
Injected into frozen arms.
Hugged tight!

Snuggled,
sensual moment.
Moist flesh blazing jointly.
Humored by the sticky embrace.
Focused!

My Yellow Flower

Privileged by your presence.
Yellow flower in eyes!
Beautiful and pleasant.
Yellow flower surprise!
Visually soft essence.

Shining ever so bright.
Yellow flower shower!
Fulfilling a good life.
Yellow flower power!
Source of a guiding light.

Governing true beauty.
Yellow flower sparkles!
Cinematic movie.
Yellow flower marvel!
My attractive cutie.

So, You Say

$\mathcal{Y}$ou say don't lie to me,
    but you tell lies to my face.
You watch me like a television,
    then scheme to manipulate financial gains.
You lust upon those who can't see you,
    or know what you are scheming.
You point out my flaws,
    and continuously ignore yours.
You smile in my face,
    yet talk about me behind my back.

IAN

*P*owers — fierce Florida storm,
Cold rain, and strong wind.
I hope Ian ends sooner.

Spelling

*P*oetic wordplay!
Resonating ambience,
plus, higher learning.

Anointed

Inspiration from Emily Dickenson's "There is Another Sky"

*U*nder the blue **sky**.
Timing moments that are **fair**.
Compared to highlights of **sunshine**.
Remembering the days I was **there**.
Wind flowing across **fields**.
Trees growing inside **forests**.
Grass is emerald **green**.
Alongside an abundant **garden**.
Outlined by colorful **flowers**.
Throat pushes out a peaceful **hum**.
Alto-Voice resembles my **brother**.
Anticipating his presence shall **come**.

Spicy Chicken

*W*arm temperatures at 350 degrees
bake slowly for an hour in olive oil,
soft and tender to bite and chew with ease.
Sometimes might add water for a little boil,
seasoned with perfect spices flavor last
Prepared, and cooked in a disposable pan.
Blends of cracked pepper, onions, garlic, and Ms. Dash.
Tongs are used to flip instead of a bare hand.
Aromatic smell layered on the salad,
instant gratification on taste buds,
Delicious to taste on top of your palate.
This particular meat I always love,
The crave is a urge envisioned during sleep at night
even others smile with so much delight.

The Microphone

*S*tage or studio
Tool used in music
Rap slang and argot
It's therapeutic
Wordplay overflow

Perfect time to shine
Perform metaphors
Stimulate the mind
Wireless or chords
Clever lines and rhymes

Grooves are fast or slow
Vocals and lyrics
Pros craft crowd control
Consistently prolific
Poetry from soul

My Pen Sounds Like Mozart

Accurate precision when gliding soft strokes,
thoughts of passion tattoo sheets of paper
expressing experiences for a favor.
Perfect melodies captured in music notes
synchronized tones delivering rhythm...
classic to ear, a sound where horns whistle,
written orchestra the color of nickel.
An automatic constant free system,
the drum sounds like inhaling deep within.
Topics are tasteful mental massages;
soul-driven revelations spoken honestly.
The zone reminds me of a time long back then.
Consistent poetry openly written
a personal passage that says, listen!

The Actor

*E*ach transformation,
leads to another word.
Signifying the adaptation,
convincing expressions.
Juggling body language,
that portrays a given image.
Time assists in proper discipline.
Orchestrating a presence,
a presence psychologically relevant.
Creating silent space,
of the developed energy.
Energy suited for specific characters,
driven by talent.
Defining useful methods.
Globally connected!

World Within a World Within a World

$\mathcal{L}$ooking out of such powerful capsule;
    As the beast struggles to digest,
    thoughts of blue are the prized asset.
Inside working each task at hand steadily channeled!

Grounded on a stationary plane of freedom;
    Never a spectator in a battle for justice,
    soundly connected to that eternal oneness.
Knowing the victory of defeat is yet to be won!

Harmonized amongst a community beneath a brown shell;
    Scribing survival sunlight admires,
    floating off as mind erases razor wires.
Enjoying life in heaven even under the hammered nails!

Eyes applaud such disciplined glow of fire;
    Returning light to every untamed ego,
    pacifying the rowdy will of hopelessness that grows.
Refilling that centered passion the soul desires!

When The Fog Cleared...

When the fog cleared –
The silence of happiness roared in a wind of peace.
leaving the past moments, never forgotten,
All the miles of pain deep within felt rotten.
Along that journey, uphill big, as a mountain!
Time, patience, and I joined as a force in spirit.
While faith sat on a cloud waiting to rain,
It seemed really strange how long it took for things to change.
Out of nowhere hope from a seed,
grew up into a strong flower.
I can never count the hours, already.
I've lived with this power.
The trees waved as I passed.
Sometimes I even saw them laugh.
Content was just half of what really made them glad.
My presence being a humble vehicle of energy,
moved through foggy challenges that opposed.
And as soon as the bitterness from depression was gone,
the doors of entrapment were no longer closed.

Reading Declare Artistry

*E*verything has a decree,
comprehend and have success.
It's the key to being free.

Three-Two

Consciously confident, collecting creations — check
Trusting time-lapse, taken truly — test

Working writer, wishing wonder — why
Focused forward fitting faster — fly

Building bigger broader blessings — before
After anger assemble around — allure

... Namsayin!

T here is a cool spirit lady that works in a movie theater.
Her heart was so big that when the last movie was about to
play, she unlocked the entrance door for a hard-working man.

He showed his appreciation by bowing his head and
shaking her hand..... *Namsaying!*

Moments after several footsteps, he turned and asked
her name. Her response was,
"I thought you'd never ask... *Namsaying!*"

She then followed up by asking him what movie
he was going to see. He replied, Wakanda!
She quickly blurted out, "man that's a good one,
it's on my to do list too ... *Namsaying!*"

He smiled and stated it was his third time seeing it.
She busted out laughing.
He said, "dang!... *Namsaying!*"

He invited her in to watch it with him.
She said no,
I'm still on the clock and could get fired.

Cleverly he asked,
"if she'd be willing to get him some popcorn,
and he'd give her a cash tip". She didn't hesitate and told him
she could use some extra gas money.

She showed up to his seat with a drink and popcorn.
The theater was empty

and he demanded she stay and watched it with him.
She did! Soon after into the movie
she began eating up the popcorn. He giggles, with a funny response
"I could have bought your own... *Namsaying!*"

She immediately turned and looked at him. He did the same.
She asked, why are you
looking at me like that?... *Namsaying!*"

He began moving in slowly for a kiss...... *Namsaying!*"

The Coiffeur

*F*irst day,
Will you help me?
My mind scampers rapid
action talks more than words, so yes!
Ready?

Clearly,
it's been ten years.
Working barber clippers,
but I'm up for a quick challenge.
Haircuts?

Let's go.
Alcohol! Towel!
Also, razor! Black comb!
working magic, both hands contain blessings,
no lie.

Slowly!
Gliding across
upper portioned hair lengths,
then down alongside temples and nape.
Any guard.

Constant,
barber training.
Enrolled, Irwin Tech School.
Amount of months, nineteen evenings.
Graduate!

I learned,
proper cleaning,
temp-fade, skin fade, beard shave
shampoo, point cuts, and other techniques.
Polished!

Job search!
Salary success.
Brown chair, the new connects.
Earning customer service respect,
seasoned!

Business!
Month lease agreement,
over-head, supplies, taxes
managed, focused, daily phone calls,
and texts.

Indeed!
Without short cuts.
Unless fuzzy long strands
of black, silver gray, curly, or straight
needs it.

Tactics!
Involve fresh trends,
desired by the person.
Even loss hairs replaced with dark
fibers.

Man piece!
Bald head cleanings.
Precise sticky sealant!
Results adopt perfect new look,
Repeat.

Each one!
Doctors, Surgeons!
Use my service frequent.
Dating years back; to operate
top-notch!

Self

Mirror! Mirror! On the wall!
Every day I rush to my favorite place.
To miss a day could bring on illness.
The fun embraced, a gaze at the face.

So many single black strands of hair.
They bunch together, and curl each way.
Postured firm with no despair.
As my days grow old, and still no signs of gray.

Those brown round eyes.
To help complement my feature.
Lashes are dark, long, and wide.
Another of the world's most interesting creatures.

The wide-angled nose,
helping enhance a keener sense.
Projected artistically composed.
Perfection at work and don't need another inch.

Such natural full lips.
Important to the unified body.
It talks, smiles, eats and spits.
Most important attractive features probably.

Suddenly a pain from a shattered mirror,
a shattered mirror of pain suddenly!
Suddenly a pain from a shattered mirror,
a shattered mirror of pain suddenly!

Follow Your Heart

$\mathcal{T}$he power of influence is a gift filled with potential, moving to- ward greater success. It creates a sense of reliability that balances trusting the process. Leading from within eliminates the disturbance of fear and opportunity prevention. There are numerous roadblocks aligned to detour our goals for making progress. Even though many opportunities are missed, following your heart at- tracts the rewards of an abundant harvest, it opens up doors un- imagined and secures organized life management.

There is power in listening from within and unifying intuition. The chemistry gels the perfect blend building up enough courage to follow the guidance provided by a leading heart. Without the distraction of ego, criticism, or judgment, honest movement creates a personal urge to attract opportunity. Can you remember a time when you made plans to go somewhere, then after entertaining a conversation with a friend who recommended going somewhere different, you changed your mind to go with them? Then later, you witness results of regret because of the choice not to follow your own heart. Bringing life into the thought of not knowing what blessings were waiting ahead wishing that you would have just shown up. That idea can be haunting.

Opportunity knocks on the door of chance fueled by courage. Timing is everything. Who can know when to be at the perfect place at the right time? Sometimes, it takes a little act of stepping outside the box to create better opportunities. My very own experience started when I was contacted by the publisher of my first poetry book requesting I sign up for a book display at three different conference events as a package deal. The cost of the three-event package deal was above my budget but I didn't let that stop me.

One of the events was at a location near where I lived, the other two weren't. So, I called the location near me to ask if I can attend the event even though I am not a publishing company. I was told yes, as an author I can sign up to come in and attend the event as long as I pay the individual ticket price. I did not hesitate to travel there for the experience of learning what that particular conference was about. The minute I arrived at the conference, the feeling felt like it was the right thing I should be doing and the type of place I needed to be.

Everybody has the option of choices. The result may or may not be what is expected but the practice of its consistency eventually creates accuracy. The accuracy formulates a core of confidence when making decisions. For example, the above experience stemmed from information about the American Library Association 2016 Conference, and acting on a decision of going to see what it was all about. The result led to meeting people for networking purposes, learning what opportunities were available to authors, and taking the initiative to promote my book. In my eyes, attending the conference was a success because of the learning experience. It boosted my confidence levels of trust when following my heart. It is because of following my heart that I may have made the right contact for my second poetry book.

Impartial Portrait

In My Opinion (Why do people get divorced?)

In my opinion, it could be because one of the two individuals
or both, was not mature enough to be honest in the beginning.

It's the beginning that will determine how valuable
the timespan of the relationship and its defined meaning.

In my opinion, it could be the lack of communication
triggered by intellectual inferiority involving numerous topics.

It's certain topics that interfere with psychological judgment
causing a stimulation in the ego or self – esteem.

In my opinion, it could be those childhood habits
that is more favorable than your significant other.

It's your significant other that deserves first priority
versus a second or third choice.

In my opinion, it could be those continuous unnecessary
spending tendencies and purchases.

It's the purchasing of items that doesn't equate to
what is relevant when juggling a tight budget.

Get While the Good is Still Getting

Life is too short, sometimes rest is no consideration.
It's facts that support next level advancements,
the offspring of an accelerated drive.

Dreaming of sleep, monitoring the distance of
exhausted bones and flesh. Athletically refreshed!
From gulps of my favorite mixed berry Celsius.

Pulled from multiple angles each demanding 100%
Patiently dividing time and energy balanced equally.
Stressing a better result.

Longing for exercise to massage the mental and blood circulation.
Ducking heart attacks and strokes.
Pressing nerves that put pressure on blood vessels. What a strain!

Yet! Still, I move Forward to conquer more than less.
Acting on an invested tomorrow,
settled upon the sacrifice today.

Life is too short, sometimes rest is no consideration.
It's facts that support next level advancements,
the offspring of an accelerated drive.

Words from external observations lack comprehension.
However, I embrace the concern and remain open-minded.
Building a shield of energy that repels negativity.

Eyesight centered on a clear forward vision.
Deaf to all else, sound has no presence.
Blind to irrelevance, sight has no blur.

Believing no other option compares to
understanding luck is as consistent as the Lottery.
The greatest wins are founded upon hard work.

Truth or Square

So, is it true? Is jealousy and envy evil?
For they are best friends with lazy minds.
A conspiracy theory taking action upon the most vulnerable.
The get-over approach camouflaged as an associate or friend.
A situation, where the innocent lose.
Just imagine if wealth and other valuables are involved,
it seems trickery is the master of deceit.
Now, this plague terrorizes many minds across the globe.
Normal to any insane mind, aggravating
to the majority who become victims.

Transitions

*L*iving life as a boy consists of dealing with issues and situations that are interesting to an audience observing up close or at a distance. Many stages of growth require practice to help mature certain characteristics that need to develop. Becoming a man incorporates learning about habits that are unhealthy. Then, taking action to become disciplined enough to control it.

Living life as a boy consists of dealing with issues and situations interesting to an audience observing up close or at a distance. Accepting the reality that most things in life rarely stay the same proves that there is a process occurring that permits change. And becoming a man, solidify inner strength built from personal choices. Then walking confidently in an honorable manner many admire.

Living life as a boy consists of dealing with issues and situations interesting to an audience observing up close or at a distance. It happens so quickly for life is too short. Some memories reflect growth uniquely. Immature thoughts most times appear due to lacking enlightenment. Loud ways and actions are untamed before civilized.

Be mindful of your actions, sometimes what you do can be misleading. Especially when you are not doing it intentionally. But it's your choice just know that you may not like what follows. It's called responsibility; we all have it.

Honestly

*H*onestly, it's my fault!
And that's the reason
I point the finger at myself.

The days as a child innocently fearful of
what the consequences will be — I told a lie.

Honestly, it's my fault!
And that's the reason
I point the finger at myself.

When in school I decided to do other things
instead of studying — I did not get the grades I wanted.

Honestly, it's my fault!
And that's the reason.
I point the finger at myself.

Making the choice to use my bill money to engage in various
activities for fun — my debt issues increased.

Honestly, it's my fault!
And that's the reason
I point the finger at myself.

Obviously, the intimate relationship I have is not enough so I
pursued another intimate encounter — I got caught.

Honestly, it's my fault!
And that's the reason.
I point the finger at myself.

Health declining after years of drinking and smoking.
Day in and day out without remorse — serious damage now exists.

Honestly, it's my fault!
And that's the reason
I point the finger at myself.

Attitude so distasteful to the point that when talking with others,
it reflects soon as the conversation is not going as intended — turn off.

Honestly, it's my fault!
And that's the reason
I point the finger at myself.

The drive to succeed is everyone's calling just as long as the internal
    decision
allows that initial step to move forward and never give up —
    perseverance.

Honestly, it's my fault!
And that's the reason
I point the finger at myself.

What Do You Do?

What do you do?
When you meet a person tested by the many challenges,
camouflaged as a bad habit such as yourself?
It always makes sense to share an uplifting thought
that might motivate them in a way unimagined.

Sometimes, we meet people
who are generous enough to share words
that click the switch turning light bulbs on.
Clearing the fog, so the eyes and mind
can see that there is light at the end of the tunnel.

Breathing life into redundant ways of living,
unfavorable to reaching greatness.
Open minds receive in a way
symbolic to the less fortunate
extending hands in hopes of cuddling autarky.

Growing an awareness strong enough to disfigure
destructive uniforms ironed to wear.
Carefully, boasting about the new pair of spectacles
an injected jealousy in Cartier frames.
Feel the power you generate! Love what you build!

What do you do?
When you meet a person tested by the many challenges,
camouflaged as a bad habit such as yourself?
It always makes sense to share an uplifting thought
that might motivate them in a way unimagined.

You Thought...

$\mathcal{Y}$ou see, it was all good in the beginning
when you thought, that which you received
was sincerely given from the heart.

It happened so much you became spoiled.
You began to rely on this habit.
Training your belief of such expectation
to where nothing else mattered
because you were overwhelmed!

The eyes became blind to the hidden agendas.
The spirit you were attracted to became a turn-off.
The love you allowed to grow sporadically,
slowly transitioned from happiness to fear.
Your self-esteem crawled beneath the darkest shadows.

Words rolled off the tongue as a stutter.
Nerves within the body shivered beside painful impulses.
Health declined below normal standards.
Now, the mind is confused and missing.
Your center is unbalanced.

The feeling is a mirror image of prison,
trapped in a space with no way out.
Emotionally violated beyond the worst imagination
crying for freedom.

Yet still, sleeping with the enemy.
All because, it was good in the beginning
when you thought, that which you received
was sincerely given from the heart.

When Laughter Cry

*N*ever a dull moment...
so many things, so many places,
so many eyes mirror lakes.

So much affliction,
floating inside veins.
The question remains...

When the mystery exists,
the wickedness permits?
May the force protect!

Ignorance Diminished

My pursuit of your happiness,
brings me to the understanding fact
of a conscious moment realizing our truth.

Driven by my spirit's necessary point,
attached to the open mind and willpower.
My mental exercise relatively anoints,
rising to a higher-self-grown flower.

Minus confusion, minus distractions,
and accepting all phases in development.
Designing a greater whole, no fractions.
Ignorance diminished into common sense.

Nonstop and deliberate intention.
Heard through action, my mouth never mentioned.

One Step Ahead

$\mathcal{Y}$ou say don't lie to me,
>   but you tell lies to my face.
You watch me like a television,
>   then scheme to manipulate financial gains.
You lust upon those who can't see you,
>   or know what you are doing.

The New

$\mathcal{L}$ife is much different from the traditional way of doing things.
There is new technology that operates at unimaginable speeds.
    Feels like the presence of people is slowly disappearing.

What took me days to finish on a typewriter,
now it only takes me a few minutes.
    Life has advanced in a way that makes the eye blind.

The true challenge is that of comprehension.
Learning this new way of life promotes loneliness.
    The savvy have no problem; their world is new.

It is the computer that I am talking about!
Online communication and universal networking,
    a new love accepted and embraced.

Conversations are occurring at long distances.
More business sales and services increasing,
    all operated from a chair within the homes of people.

Worldwide evolution has spread this disease.
The only question sitting in the minds of many,
    is this for better or worse?

Superficial

*T*he life of luxury is your outline.
A design of perfection I cherish.
Occupy my space, and share what is Divine.
Release the beheld, passion is jealous.
Lay your mind on my heart, I answered thought.
Silently absorbed freely as nature.
Intense response ignored before caught,
blessed in a sense for us to gain favor.
Relatively important above the flesh,
rooted deeply awakens strong spirits.
Marking territory spiritually wet,
encircled energy beyond limits.
Climax the social-net engulfed respect,
intended purpose traveling progress.

Fallen Bridge

*T*he tumbling starts,
slowly in rhythmic strides.
How will I survive the strong tides?
Bank credit is high,
way above the limit!
Wait a minute, I'm not finished:
car payments for two months are
behind going on its third.
Car insurance is now canceled,
jeopardizing the driver's license.
That gets me from point "A" to point "B",
confusing since I'm working two jobs.
Sometimes, even three
locations are the places for me.
Hours decreasing, minimizing pay!
All I can say is the challenge is tough every day.
Analyzing and restructuring my resume,
while seeking permanent positions.
Doing everything I can to change this condition.
Verbally expressed my professional skills,
photographer slash videographer.
Just to express the many hurdles,
I'm expected to jump and hop over.

Spinning Wheels

*T*ested by fate
longing escape
running in such
rat race

The mental
draws thoughts
like pens
or pencils
by each individual

Digging deep
awake or sleep
to extend
a higher reach
well above 7 feet

Free from land
the ultimate plan
grow and expand
a greater demand
all because it can

Soaked within
close as friends
it never ends
when the circle spin
time begins

Inner City Kids

Inner city kids!
Live their best lives.
Puzzled by mediocrity,
yet find ways from nothing.

Inner city kids!
Growing up unaccustomed to material riches.
Countered filled wealthy spirits,
yet a heart too big to hold.

Inner city kids!
Laugh in the arms of family.
Cry with heads in supportive chests,
yet sings happy songs that free pain.

Inner city kids!
Experience social connectivity.
Embrace personal differences,
and learn true love.

Inner city kids!
Attracted to sports and music.
Master gifts abound,
and wish to be greater

Inner city kids!
Travel within their hometown.
Glow a fascinating presence,
and project a power of confidence.
Inner city kids!

Fatherhood

Hold up! Time out! It's a must I step away for a moment from this conversation. It's evident my tolerance level is at its tipping point, you see, the steam is ready to blow? Wait! Are you still talking? Now I must remove myself, excuse me. I'll be in the bathroom disarming anger and regaining my higher sense of self.

So many times, I've been working so hard to keep tight grips on the ball I call fatherhood. I'd prefer you as my better half to allow me a position on the team other than stereotypical expectations. So, can I please share and voice my opinion now?

I'm well aware that I may or may not be the biological father. Listen here, we both chose to allow the privilege of wearing these shoes. I'd rather have your respect and consider some of the ideologies I'm bringing forth. Our kids may find the information useful to an extent.

Hold up! Time out! It's a must I step away for a moment from this conversation. It's evident my tolerance level is at its tipping point, you see the steam is ready to blow? Wait! Are you still talking? Now I must remove myself, excuse me. I'll be in the bathroom disarming anger and regaining my higher sense of self.

New Jersey Winter Tides

I remember clearly, the memory is my everyday story.
Living in the city walking home during winter nights.
Day after day, leaving basketball practice at my Catholic School.

My body embraces the grip of my Cleveland Browns starter jacket.
Deflecting a winter breeze, so I am warm.

My Feet bounce around inside a boot, one size too big.
Hurting from the cold that scatters my skin.

My eyes before blurry from the liquid tears puddled comfortably.
As my face splashes against such fierce resistance.

My lips smile at the beauty of it all.
Working in a collaborative effort towards my numbness.

My eardrums dissect sounds matching.
The light dancing along treetops.

When It All Started

*W*hen it all started.......

I honestly believe it was a combination of many different things
contributing to my unfavorable results.

When it all started.......

The home I considered home, I loved so much
it became an irritable allergy to my focus and goals.

When it all started.......

Recollection search for any form of abuse,
to stimulate subconscious replay.

When it all started.......

Reacting in a way that makes no sense.
Nowhere to blame, and no excuses.

When it all started.......

Dinkum Proclivity

Unembellished Notion

Sophisticated simple attraction!
Non-impressive superficial belief,
magnetically drawn to better sweets.
Comfortable within its silky satin,
grounded enough to keep pinched hearts laughing.
Chasing opposites clinging to the weak,
training strength to hold firm as a tree leaf.
Pragmatism influx just a fraction!
It's the simple things that means so much more,
blessed to us finding their better behalf.
Qualifying is a value adore.
Forward and direct is a trustful mask.
No day or time together is a bore,
if you don't know, communicate and ask.

Secret Rendezvous

Silence smoothers safe space within leaf-like soaking flavor.
Thoughts burst inside mental, colored apples showing flavor.

Adored answers about angles useful to write lyrics.
Reminds of time mental constraints prefer slowing flavor.

Bringing boundless beloved brightness engulfed in arms, honey.
Upon steaming almonds creamed milk brownish smoking flavor.

Calling! Conscious control center drinking sober liquor.
Karma's keen eye observes good vibes. Embrace rolling flavor!

Scented sugar solid sparkle caress tongue tip palates.
Trepid to taste impressed stiff ego, open stroking flavor.

Endless extracts engage easy intimate valued content.
Author submerged deeply! Writing challenge noting flavor.

Cold Room

The genius I am, surely proved true.
So many days sharing space in a place I never knew.
Alone with thoughts dancing rhythm's corybantic pulse.
Confident my happy day memories match the test results.
My arms embraced, palms and fingertips.
Rubbing goosebumps, feeling cold air, along with chap lips.
Laying on my back, staring at bland walls.
Awaiting my entitlement, to make a phone call.
Cut off from the nobility and Godly privilege.
Reading and writing more to keep from being discouraged.

These Three Words....just the thought of it!

These Three Words....just the thought of!

$\mathcal{P}$lace us at the seat of a connection unfamiliar to touch.
Tranquilized by the seeping soliloquy visually.
Apprentice in our engagement entertaining multiple contractions,
acting out what is internal, for flesh holds no deliverance.

These Three Words....just the thought of!

$\mathcal{R}$ight and exact, one with the act of knowing your worth.
Tolerating those compliments continually addressed.
Caressed beneath your bosoms, clamoring the theme of each heartbeat.
Triggered by the vigorous impulse laminated signature.

These Three Words....just the thought of!

$\mathcal{P}$enetrating the soul, persisting the push for ecstasy.
Imagining what the experience feels like having your soul next to me.
The unison is a power greater than repetitive earthquakes,
even trembling after vibrations move the body,

These Three Words....just the thought of!

$\mathcal{E}$levates the passion embedded in every stroke of our wings.
Remembering this life marks that forever theme.
Enjoying soft whispers stimulating enchantment.
Laughing does us well! Each moment in time reveals.

It's Okay

You are beautiful!
Become one with your talents,
enjoy your freedom.

Dream killers are evil,
they attract what's negative.
Focus hard – prevail!

The source is a gift,
for lust breeds the envy and hate.
Therefore, vanquish such actions.

Revive self- leverage.
Stack positive endeavors,
avoid them at all costs.

Achieve your greatness!
The blessings are plentiful,
accept and protect them.

My, My, My

My life is a poem: my daily routines act as words.
My thoughts are productive: bouncing around imitating lottery balls.
My tongue speaks positivity: people become inspired and motivated
My eyes write visions: I can see clearly a focus larger than life.
My actions conquer moments: strength prevails.
My hands manifest poetry: my work detail is an enjoyment
My poems animate vividly – hypnotic as television.
My heart boils a love: felt at a distance.
My radiation travels, with no discrimination.
My presence brings dis-ease – even the sun gets jealous.
My wings grow unique feathers – wow!
My voice harmonizes words – that facilitates productive impact.
My mind is an arena – harvesting the brightest stars.
My path is one of a kind, similar feet match the vibrations.

Rapture

Lush, bonfire moments!
Massaged and caressed gently.
Two bouncing heartbeats!

Dignity professed!
Permanently bonded oath.
A connected fate!

Acknowledged foresight!
Premeditated feelings.
Drowning emotions!

Newfangled Culmination

*T*he culmination of internal beauty,
flows deeper that the superficial.
It has no attitude attached – moody!
Sometimes matches the artistic flesh- physical.

My mind races rapidly toward a second me.
A day one longing for the opposite sex.
A suit dressed down in trust – free!
The facts are clear, there's no hypothetical guess.

Fraudulent impressions are absent at the moment.
Past encounters were only experience and practiced.
The present embraces confidence in motion,
in preparation to advance into a supreme classic.

Potting patience to get a greater castle,
laughing at chaos in abundance.
Assisted living through life's battles,
winning attitudes blatantly pungent.

Forever invested without loss of self.
The truth is, what you see is what you get.
Comfortable in the journey without being hard felt.
Sincere in the person I own at best.

Personal Standards

*E*verybody has that one fantasy, there's no exception to the rule;
    It could be that you are attracted to natural hair,
      obtaining the most profound smell within the nostrils.

The eyes' inner glow connects with the soul,
    embracing life's experiences attached to memory.

The perfect shape that outlines human existence,
    stimulating nature until the craving is persistent.

The intellectual cells that transport messages,
    of formulated thoughts and words released in sound.

The pearl-coated teeth resonate with cleanliness,
    complementing the brightest happiness in every smile.

Or the softest reflection of any complexion,
    where the flow of its freedom is pure as water.

Everybody has that one fantasy, there's no exception to the rule;
    It could be that you are attracted to natural hair,
      obtaining the most profound smell within the nostrils.

Nothing Else Compares

It's something simple, nothing else compares.
For the thoughts that you think are unique.
The words you speak are hypnotizing.
The sights you see are alluring.
The smells inhaled are refreshing.

You're everything I need to assist my journey.
The connection is strong and radiating.
The world is a challenge waiting for us to experience.
All is good, Yes! All is good the finest design,
and a classic memory is never forgotten.

Silhouette of a Fervent Esquire

I hear loud phone ringing Barred Owl tunes, white-Collar hard work.
Unique undone utter, unfolds acts of counsel efforts.

Naïve vision distorts yellow hallways walking forward.
Neutral notice never narrates presumed blue-collar comfort,

Except under unique radars geared to legal casework.
Lawyers' limbic language lessons reflect perfect, expert!

Very clever leader engaged, helping freedom evolve.
Instincts involve insight into darker color outbursts.

Spinning spirals coded with a bluish rubber clothed wheel.
Increased intrigue indeed inspires reddish hotter pressures.

Office hours screaming absurd amounts of unknown overtime.
Namely noble naïve numbers beyond dollars' true worth.

Vogue Embroidery

Summer daylight slides through open windows, country Kansas.
Early essence explains elder spunky new trend practice.

Artist working alone using constant machine focus,
making master methods memoirs inside, very own Palace.

Shadows witness steady progress provokes fervor emotions,
thinking towards trendy textures that do surpass average.

Ruby glowing silk threads brandished atop, clearly noticed.
Engaged effort explores enriched gorgeous dark mint fabrics.

Simple soft-tip garments arranged in ways appraised opus.
Stunning stitches speaking stories about thin hemmed graphics.

Expounds deeper into designs at that unique moment,
sturdy satin symbols sizzle designs on blank canvas.

Communal Sentiment

Turn Down the Temperature

Anger boils a nasty hatred.
Making it difficult to express,
acting without thinking, building up stress.

Unknown attacks upon American Citizens...
What is considered innocent is now a victim?
Questioning Why? And who is killing them?

The root and cause is a continuous dispute.
Between equal justice and fair human rights,
pushing towards color barriers that take one's life.

The rich! The poor! The majority ignored.
Who's presence is vulnerable and unprotected.
There goes that bullet again – unexpected!

Accountability

$\mathcal{Y}$et still people are being killed.
And all I am seeing or hearing about are people whose outer lining
    contains serious traces of melanin.

This is no racial statement or prejudicial empowering soliloquy.
Their guns blast quicker than accumulated memberships within
the National Rifle Association.

Yet still people are being killed.
And all I am seeing or hearing about are people whose outer lining
    contains serious traces of melanin.

This is no racial statement or prejudicial empowering soliloquy.
Their guns blast quicker than any political protest against legally
undoing the Tiahrt Amendment.

Yet still people are being killed.
And all I am seeing or hearing about are people whose outer lining
    contains serious traces of melanin.

This is no racial statement or prejudicial empowering soliloquy
Their guns blast quicker than the mind assuming death is in the air
lacking probable cause.

Yet still, people are being killed.
And All I am seeing or hearing about are people whose outer lining
    contains serious traces of melanin.

This is no racial statement or prejudicial empowering soliloquy.
Their guns blast quicker than the excuses defined as justifiable
homicide.

Yet still people are being killed.
And All I am seeing or hearing about are people whose outer lining
contains serious traces of melanin.

This is no racial statement or prejudicial empowering soliloquy.
Their guns blast quicker than new life created, doing it the first time.

Yet still people are being killed.
And All I am seeing or hearing about are people whose outer lining
contains serious traces of melanin.

This is no racial statement or prejudicial empowering soliloquy.
Their guns blast quicker than hunting season, aiming at ducks and
deer.

Yet still people are being killed.
All I am seeing or hearing about are people whose outer lining
contains serious traces of melanin.

This is no racial statement or prejudicial empowering soliloquy.
Their guns blast quicker than an ignorant mind responding to a
topic just to argue.

Yet still people are being killed.
All I am seeing or hearing about are people whose outer lining
contains serious traces of melanin.

This is no racial statement or prejudicial empowering soliloquy.
Their guns blast quicker than a blinded mind ready for the inevitable.

There Goes That Bullet Again

All lives matter but right now I'm focused on the lives of
those filled with a serious amount of melanin attached
to their outer shell.

Whether it is or isn't discrimination,
they are flooding the population spontaneously.

There goes that bullet again...

Unexpectedly, the innocent suffers,
gasping for their last breath.
Their last breath that life will bear witness.

Whether it is or isn't racism,
they are flooding the population spontaneously.

There goes that bullet again...

All lives matter but right now I'm focused on the lives of
those filled with a serious amount of melanin attached
to their outer shell.

Whether it is or isn't prejudice,
they are flooding the population spontaneously.

There goes that bullet again...

Solving the problem, resolution, yes!
That is what the people want.
The people want life and community safety.

Whether it is or isn't discrimination,
they are flooding the population spontaneously.
There goes that bullet again!
There goes that bullet again!
There goes that bullet again!

Reminded

Our past is always reminded of the future.
It feels like today is no different from yesterday.
Fires burn churches and buildings ferociously.
South Carolina and North Carolina specifically.
Childish behavior animated abroad.
Hidden in daylight, unseen, pure disrespect.

Our past is always reminded of the future.
It feels like today is no different from yesterday,
the laws we fought for are continuously countered cleverly.
The lives taken are adding up.
A color unfavorable to some with different shades of skin.
The journey endured we face, ignorance reincarnated.

Our past is always reminded of the future.
It feels like today is no different from yesterday.
Justice sits in the hands of question.
So many minds ponder this destruction.
So many spirits are haunted.
Puzzling even though we all know the answer.

Our past is always reminded of the future.
It feels like today is no different from yesterday.
Fires blaze resembling that of casteism.
Prejudice dressed in a bleached sheet.
Hate at a handicap targeting those weak and innocent.
A stimulus of retaliating impulses inside nature's veins.

Our past is always reminded of the future.
It feels like today is no different from yesterday.

There is always a bigger picture.
What is the cause of this effect?
The power of ego is so dangerous.
The fear of a jealous heart whines inside.

Recidivism: Pulmonary Embolism

*H*abitual is an inconspicuous tattoo exploring the less favorable,
defying the odds, and contradicting what factors flourish.
There's destruction that loiters, urban communities in abundance.
A system triggered by malfunction, let the emendation commence!
When the facts unfold an imbalance circumvents program initiatives.
So, we focus on second chances and rehabilitation.

Paying close attention to the most effective forms of rehabilitation,
hoping the best sources surface and are considered favorable.
It all begins with lining up the best initiatives,
and documenting statistics to guarantee results that flourish.
Burglary and robbery are the highest, let the emendation commence.
The number of men and women entering the cycle is in abundance.

The massive number of returning offenders into prison in abundance.
Sometimes, it's a harder fight for effective rehabilitation.
Prior records become the new popular let the emendation commence.
Tallying ages between teens and mid-'20s is high-favorable.
Loss of focus because employment challenges flourish.
Repeated criminal activity sparks new goal initiatives.

The lack of goal setting that will stamp on productive initiatives.
Rule out precautionary exercises, bullet points used in abundance,
entertaining personal meetings is a safe space to help flourish.
Facilitate the mentally traumatized for separate rehabilitation,
determining what percentage of a particular crime is favorable.
Institutionalized mentalities, let the emendation commence.

Restrictions of supervised emancipation, the emendation commence.
The number of habitual returns from prison is in abundance.
Contemplating if societal interpersonal relationships will flourish.
Adding effective education to guarantee affordable rehabilitation.
Trusting the process so more results are favorable.
There's a thin line between sobriety and preventative initiatives.

Affiliations can be a present factor in some ex-offender's initiatives.
Progression over regression, let the emendation commence.
Issuing monitored engagements applying curriculums that's favorable.
Using preparation and support teams to spread love in abundance.
Tracking the estimated individual participation in rehabilitation.
Involving various community elites to flourish.

Identifying favorable elements to make better decision in abundance.
Carefully dissecting initiatives of growth that continue and commence.
Self-rehabilitation of an autodidact person will flourish.

Now Texas: 5 Lives!

All lives matter, even police officers.
So many lives are taken by gun violence.
So many eyes cry and no more silence.

Next could be teachers, accountants, and lawyers.
World peace America and Middle East,
too much war along with differences.
Too much ignorance and deaf ears listening.

Protest demonstrations, people flooding streets...
Solutions are needed to destroy hate.
What change reminds us how to calm the fuse?
What changed laws, fair justice, and media news?
The past, now present spreading state to state.

Circulating at a fast rate each year anew.
Dialogue and debates, yet still, no clue.

What is going on?

What a plague! I mean there is really a serious dis – ease
going on throughout the nation.
It's so contagious and becoming uncontrollable,
traveling from state to state.
Picking out the bodies of a human beings,
most are young with a future.

One root of the cause is problematic.
It is the source of action using unnecessary excessive force.
An equation that equals injustice,
and still so many lives are taken.
The number grows – sporadic
Ignoring is a contribution,
for ignorance increases the pain.
So, the question still remains-
What is going on?

Solid: The Other Part of the Story

What a relief from the ultimate restriction.
A psychological knot loosened. I'm amazed!
Left leg pierced. Could've bled to death.
Life feels so good when survival calls.
Detained and restrained, contained based on circumstantial.
Trusting a trial court will serve justice.
Trusting a Grand Jury and twelve jury.
Falling short with a public defender – convicted.
Sentenced to 120 months served in prison.
Endured the paper fight receiving numerous denials.
Finally released to regain all lost valuables.
Focused on the process of living against odds.
Rehabilitation in a manner from self-motivation.
I gradually learned how to love self, more.
Yet! I'm still alone. My little world
So, I will write about my many talents.
So, I work to match my age expectations.
My growth defies the impossible. I overcame it!
Ignoring systematic failures of a habitual offender.
Destined to mimic airplanes. Place to place!
My reality is a contradiction to recidivism.
My reality destroys that stereotype and depiction.
I believe! My faith is deep rooted – lineage.
It's a power held. The hateful witness.
For the journey continues, reversing old statistics.

Tearful: Orlando Nightclub Massacre

*T*ogether the prayers compliment so many tears in the eyes of
families.
Voices scream, "Stop taking the lives of America's Innocent".
Hearts were broken after the Zimmerman incident.
Yet, still terror floods U.S. soil giving birth to tragedy.

Together the prayers compliment so many tears in the eyes of
families.
Reason has no cause, and it's all distasteful.
Something that the world believes is hateful.
Yet, still terror floods U.S. Soil giving birth to tragedy.

Together the prayers compliment so many tears in the eyes of
families.
Remember New York, Washington D.C., and Boston!
The memory reminds us continuously often.
Yet, still terror flood U.S. soil giving birth to tragedy

Together the prayers compliment so many tears in the eyes of
families.
Permanently marked as eyes bear witness,
wishing it all ends so life on this matter is different.
Yet, still terror floods U.S. soil giving birth to tragedy.

Together the prayers compliment so many tears in the eyes of
families.
Thankful for the prayers that act as a napkin to tears,
and medicine for all pain and hurt accumulated over the years.
Yet, still terror floods U.S. soil giving birth to tragedy.

Analytic Life Tolls

Between age and skin color
I love brothers.
Even through all the hate
that makes us war with one another.

Growing up from out the gutter
most of us had nothing.
Some of us just a little something,
the reason trouble started coming.

No excuse
can justify the amount of this abuse.
The amount of lives taken
when a trigger
squeeze and shoot.

The news keep telling it,
lies they keep selling it,
and pushing Bills to pass
containing the wrong elements.

Anger builds
when we get fed up with
innocent blood shed.
Not to mention
how they keep killing kids.

Unjustified homicides
planting fear inside the minds.
Psychological demise
living in today's times.

Wearing glasses on my eyes
just to keep from walking blind.
False prophets still believe
that it was written as a sign.

You mean to tell me,
that we still need a change!

Out of the Placenta

Mothers cry! Mothers cry!
And now we know why,
so many mothers cry...

Mothers cry for the lost lives of innocent souls!
Young and unaware of society's failings.

Mothers cry! Mothers cry!
And now we know why,
so many mothers cry...

The 1900s! The 2000s!
Compare the differences before technology!

Mothers cry! Mothers cry!
And now we know why,
so many mothers cry...

Mothers cry for man's inhumanity to man on a daily basis.
Mothers cry we hope begets a new society for ALL.

Perennially Plagued

Red flags flying aimlessly free,
teacher shortage greatly.
Unfilled positions in Florida,
calls for people hastily.
Mississippi has the highest teacher vacuity,
growing rapidly.
It seems the demand,
unfolds from STEM ironically.
Labor statistics divulge,
the last four years have decreased sadly.

Distinctive Subjection

Desirable Facsimile

I remember
the first day I got a crooked edge.
Many years young when I paid close attention to my head.
I sat confident in the chair.
The place was a little empty, hardly no one there.
My throat felt the soft touches of the neck strip
as the cape was wrapped around me fastened with a metal clip.
Followed by the rumbling of the brush bristles.
Of course, when it touched my neck it kind of tickled.

Cool Care spray puddles the Andes Masters.
The strokes were slow and I wished to go faster.
Switching between a Wahls Clipper cut that skin fades.
Carefully gliding the comb in various ways.
Handed a mirror to check my reflection.
Snapping on a guard to cut with perfection.
Lining carefully with gel and a razor.
Sometimes even water contributes a good skin layer,
getting close to finishing the loose hairs with shears.
Often called scissors I find kind of weird.

That night...

I had a super busy day working at the barbershop.
It ended after taking my clothes to a laundromat to be cleaned.
Pressed by a short time because I had a barber client to meet.
I figured I would use every bit of my time wisely with two loads.

Leaving them to wash, I'm back driving on the road.
A/C is blowing hot so now I'm sweating profusely.

Make it back to my shop to cut my client's hair.
While doing so, a walk-in client appeared
asking if I could service him.
With the kind of heart I have,
I told him I will try to squeeze him in.
And so I did.

Afterward, I darted back to the laundromat
to put my clothes in a dryer.
Long story short, the barbershop day ended
and I got my laundry.
Only to realize that it's a class night plus we have a guest.
It was a late night at the shop;
I'm running short on time before the CLI class begins.

So, I pull into a gas station parking lot,
sitting in the dark with the car running.
Not paying attention, I see the gas meter on "E".
Just when I decide to move over to a pump,
the car shuts off blocking traffic.
I paused the class for a moment and popped open my trunk.
Found a water jug, and emptied the water-filled with gas.

Poured the gas into the tank just enough so the car could start.
Pulled up to a gas pump to refill.
I missed part of the guest lecture.
Became more tired.
And was tranquilized by such a busy tiring day
that ended in darkness.
That Night!

Laptop Keyboard

*N*ever knew the amount of fun I could have
when my fingers take salsa lessons over my laptop keyboard.

The marathon begins by logging into sites that need a password,
only to come face to face with memory failure.

My next maneuver is to write it down on a sheet of paper
and experience a bad case of lost and found.

The only problem is where I wrote it down wasn't found,
and that's why I say it's like a marathon.

Because I'm forced to click the tab "Forgot Password" I tell you
this new sport keeps me fit.

Never knew the amount of fun I could have
when my fingers take salsa lessons over my laptop keyboard

Florida

*F*iestas and celebrations of educational institutions..
Fun filled experiences.
First impressions are remembered as long-lasting memories.
Farming capabilities to nourish nature's harvests,
Feeling that taste of juicy mangoes
Freedom of creativity exercising passionate art.
Flashy lifestyles blended strategically.
Fitness activities promote healthier lives.
Fathers and loving mothers exercise parenting.
Focused professionals creating better communities for all.

Football games at Florida State, Florida, Miami, Tampa Bay Stadium
Fancy restaurants served top of the line foods.
Films at movie theaters playing new releases.
Foreigners visit during cold winters.
Fantastic memories enjoying the moments at Walt Disney World.
Fire-hot days wearing humidity like soaked T-shirts.

Four central cities Tampa, Orlando, St. Petersburg, and Clearwater
Fierce Hurricanes storm occasionally.
Free city parks to loaf around and wander.
Fish with exotic features streaming blue waters.
Floating markets with available space
Forgiving houses of worship plenty and abound.
Fields that attract baseball games.
Frisbee flying days or walking dogs.
Fantastic art galleries.

More than Once (Cell Phone)

I laugh at myself simultaneously angry,
contemplating my recollection of how it all happened.
I mean a little device is so important.
Still, I find it misplaced!
Yet jarring is the fact that it was... Not once!
Not twice,
nor thrice.
To this realization,
my forehead aches daily.
So, unloading the mind of frivolities
and thoughts, reorganization and freedom
put together, surely it will help.

Reject Abuse

T here is nothing that justifies
your acceptance of being a punching bag.
At the same time, understanding equality is key.
It is not right to intentionally disrupt the relationship.

Before marriage, we talked, and after marriage we argued.
Our team turned into a competition,
ego sparked inner conflict.

Reaction to this action was a loss of control.
Nothing will heal striking such beautiful flesh.
Personally characterized as a psychological disorder,
the correction is misplaced.

Often called love, spoken blatantly
used as an excuse feeding manipulation.
Yet! Succumbing the pain, you are bleeding again.

School Days

On the first day somewhere new,class begins.
Tense expressions, glued grins.

Many options to choose friends.
Exigent decisions and interchangeable opinions.

What a place!
So much space!

Extracurricular activities,
intellectual groups, and fun festivities.

Close or distant,remain focused.
Introverted before open.

Unfamiliar and even unknown,
many hungry days.
Welcome home!

Comprehension, massive readings,
party weekends
Good old school days!

Stomach Growls: No Breaks

At the start of the day,
haircuts.
No breakfast before work,
early man syndrome.
No worries,
most clients leave satisfied.

Difficult to concentrate,
operation multi-task.
Silent in thought,
and the victim of a numb tongue.

Stomach growls,
I figured a lunch break to calm the urge.
Interception:
- visions of a crispy chicken sandwich.
- countered by a shortage of time.

Another client's appointment.
Stomach growls,
now I'm back to chips and water.

Locked in place standing.
Failed lunch attempts.
Hungry!

Another client appointment
Yet, still cutting hair.

Giving Yourself

*I*t's so many things that can happen.
When acting out of anger,
and not giving yourself a second to think.

I can remember!
The many days seeing myself,
standing in halls of confusion.
Stuck in one spot
trying to figure it out.

Then there are others!
When stuck in the halls
of exhaustion, feeling pressed
by the most intolerable.

It's so many things that can happen.
When acting out of anger,
and not giving yourself a second to think.

Worst case scenario!
Misjudging the rightful act.
An experience of all external
basically, losing-self.

Pros versus cons of the situation,
repercussions revolve around percipience:
A gain unannounced,
with the confusion diminished.

It's so many things that can happen.
When acting out of anger,
and not giving yourself a second to think.

Corona Test

*W*here I work,
 I long for fresh air.
I mean!
The clean air
is what I'm used to.
I mean!
Was used to it.
That is, until I was introduced to
a two-sided piece of cloth.
Covering half of my face.

Now my blame goes towards
this thing called – Corona.
It popped up out of nowhere!

At least,
that is what I was told.

Then here comes the research.
It revealed previous variants,
but anyway,
our present circumstances prevailed.
Bringing me back to my point!
I challenged my mind
thinking,
and questioning
if this is a stupid prank.

I mean!
To wear such a thing on my face.

I'm talking mask,
in the home,
at work,
and in public.
Does it really work?
Do they protect?
I mean!
From the virus?
I only ask,
because I was a bit vigilant about wearing one.
Ignorant for not wanting to wear one
Yet!
I still tested positive for it.
Now let's give a round of applause,
for the wonderous Corona everybody.

That is!

I'm in a time where employment is unfair to the average person.
A time where two jobs is normal.
That is, if bills are to get paid on time.

The first job arrangement may be working 8am to 5pm.
The second job arrangement is working 5:30pm until close.
That is, before scheduling shuffles things up, interrupting the process.

The first job decides to schedule later than 5pm.
The second job decides to hire more, minimizing hours and earnings.
That is, unless a better strategy manifests.

Difficulties arise aggravating life's responsibilities.
A greater challenge emotionally.
That is, if strong will and mental powers enhance.

Endurance relies on motivation to keep going.
The pressure marinates its force, using time.
That is!

Unsalubrious: Dehydrated

My confusing stomach aches.
Feels like an orange-plastic tip screwdriver
pushing deep within.

My normal mind,
thought it was just a severe
case of gas swelling up in one spot.

All occurring while playing chess.
Quenching my thirst,
with a fresh Starbucks all black coffee.

Unaware of the rapid danger of dehydration.
Yes! Those coffee spurts added up
and my water craves had an allergic reaction.

My body got fed up,
and planned a way
to take out its frustration.

That's when the alien
crystal structure,
formulated inside my kidney.

Until this particular day,
I needed to urinate
but I couldn't use the toilet..

Pain increased! Vomiting began!
All because of
an impervious kidney stone.

Basketball Tryouts Tomorrow

The big day is near,
I used the entire summer to prepare.
School is back in,
and tryouts are tomorrow.
So tomorrow,
I will rain nothing but jump shots.
Once I'm feeling hot,
meaning shoot the ball nonstop.
Matter of fact!
I better go to the basketball courts today.
I'm thinking before it gets too late for me to play.
The fellas running a 5 on 5.
And heck! I'm still in my prime.
I realize,
the time is now for me to get mine.
I'm thinking jump so high,
I touch the sky.
Yes! Mr. all city!
All pro!
I will have colleges knocking at the front door.
That is,
before my hustle ability turned up a notch.
After facing better talent,
it actually caught me off balance.
Because after the loud pop!
I lost my balance,
falling to the ground.
A little pain!
A little strain!

Must be all it is.
I tried to walk,
but my left foot moves like a slinky.
So I rushed home!
And from there to the hospital.
Just to sit a little.
No wait!
The wait is longer than I expected.
The pain grew in a bigger section through my leg.
When the nurse came I was cuddled up into a ball.
Holding the back of my ankle.
I'm thinking in my mind, thank you!
To the doctor who says it's not looking good.
Afraid to ask, "Doc, is it really that bad?"
Yes! She said,
I immediately bowed my head.
With the thought dancing in my head.
Will I be able to tryout,
at basketball practice tomorrow?

Abstract Dopamine

Personify

$\mathcal{T}$here is a difference between you and them,
your drive is honest and profound.

The walls and bridges that stand before you have no chance.
The drum of your heart is boisterous.

The passion of your achievement is a lamination,
no boundaries exist in the focused mind.

So Remote

*T*he drive is what keeps my will determined,
resembling a fire running across fields of dry weeds.
The course is a training dominantly natural,
perfect to its organic birth. Sporadic!

A diet infested with deliverance,
for the result is bathed in cold pressed coconut oil.
Drenched in refinement.
Shining forever bright huddled among tolerance.
Enveloping invested perseverance.

Anointed!
Respecting that credibility, no lie.
Awaken to understand the visual manifested.
Now, the attraction is centered on
chosen and appointed.

Open Mind

It takes a good mind to be open!
Open enough to receive the message,
when conversing face-to-face.

It takes a good mind to be open!
Open enough to have the interest to listen,
acting as a sponge for wisdom.

It takes a good mind to be open!
Open enough to contribute meaningfully,
in all, an open mind is good!

Better

I'm beginning to get better!
Looking at me can remind you
that I'm a work of art.
That confused look
It's puzzling, I know!
The things I say,
the things I do
I guess....

This shaded figure under the umbrella
stands tip of an arrow
when I pivot.
So does the arrow.
Lucky for me,
my growth is fluid.
My eardrums work as sponges
Only to become
what I always should have been.
Morally defined,
so many long days of practice.
I could never imagine
the strength behind such effort
to be better.

Delineate

*W*ork titles are only a description
of what I'm capable of,
in this world we live in.
However, it doesn't describe me.
I'm talking about the mind frame, heart, and personality.
All which are based around my particular belief.

I believe there's nothing wrong with exercising good manners.
I believe a connection to a higher power lives within us.
I believe respect for self and others is honorable.
I believe education and common sense assist with relationships.
I believe effective dialogue closes the distance to understanding.
I believe hygiene should be a mirror image of cleanliness.
I believe nothing in life is guaranteed but two things, you figure it out.
I believe love and fear are children of delicacy.
I believe anger is self's worst adversary.
I believe sugar and salt are a deadly elixir.
I believe rest is the seat to a peace of mind.
I believe happiness can be found in the simple things.

Work titles are only a description
of what I'm capable of,
in this world we live in.
However, it doesn't describe me.
 I'm talking about the mind frame, heart, and personality.
All which are based around my particular belief

The Administered Attitude

The extremities that mound surface tops,
are like bouncing bingo balls that continuously pop up.
Our only hope is the administered attitude developed
in the notes taken from each lesson.

Before us, we have amazons and deserts.
In layman terms an interesting playground we hurtle.
Daily routines become consistent,
matching habits acquired in attempts to magnify self-ability.

Graded assertions,
depict the nature of evolution igniting various transitions.
Growth depends on it to be understood as a secure roadmap.

There is a time and place for everything.
Synchronization defines its meaning,
circumventing the misapprehension that belt
visibly above skin like goosebumps.

Mind power meets up with discipline.
Parading along gradually portraying confidence.
Masking the façade!
Intentionally interrupting invaluable hoarding,
of inexact data and storage.

The extremities that mound surface tops,
are like bouncing bingo balls that continuously pop up.
Our only hope is the administered attitude developed
in the notes taken from each lesson.

The longer way, my way, a better way!

Magnified under the scope,
wrote for future notes.
Displayed and provoked,
up close from a farther distance.
Persistent in the stride,
towards (the) better times.
In mind, active for any solution it provides.
High after the low, dictating direction
created by an inspiration animated.
Patient enough to journey through the scuff
I rebel with a cause unselfishly abroad.
Viewed through pupils wide as a straw.
Applauding each memory that embraces such chemistry.
Connecting us spiritually!
Driven by this silent ambition granting permission.
To "Be" before falling submissive.

Grandfather, you are missed: Mr. Lori Legette

*T*he memories last like it was yesterday.
    Clearly, I see in my mind days when
        I was welcome in your home at all times.
The memories last like it was yesterday.
    Clearly, I see in my mind days when
        you took me to the garage with you.
The memories last like it was yesterday.
    Clearly, I see in my mind days when you and
        Grandma was watching TV.
The memories last like it was yesterday.
    Clearly, I see in my mind days when
        you always fixed a car or truck.
The memories last like it was yesterday.
    Clearly, I see in my mind days when I was
        given loose change to go to the corner store.
The memories last like it was yesterday.
    Clearly, I see in my mind days when you
        and a few uncles were cooking out on the cement grill.
The memories last like it was yesterday.
    Clearly, I see in my mind days when you let
        Uncle Rick hold the car to take me fishing.
The memories last like it was yesterday.
    Clearly, I see in my mind days when you let me
        drive the Cadillac when I got a license.
The memories last like it was yesterday.
    Clearly, I see in my mind days when you
        whooped me behind for that wrong I did.
The memories last like it was yesterday.
    Clearly, I see in my mind days when
        I didn't have the strength to attend the funeral.

My Range

My range can only be determined by what efforts enacted,
by examples of confidence proven after taking the first step.

When I do, I do it because I want to.
It's more like a matter of integrated completion.
To mistake such an identity is a limitation open for failure.

My stride is a flow of current identical to an ocean's wave
lusted upon by California's surf boarders.
The fantasy of its debut solidifies a truth beyond measure.

My range can only be determined by what efforts enacted,
by examples of confidence proven after taking the first step.

To change is a summation of the balance between
before and after. To fly is a separation between gravel
and white clouds glistening those illustrious sun rays.

So, I ask, how do I maximize the outer reflection
witnessed by the candid eye? What mechanisms contribute
towards the shift in a paradigm different from normal similarities?

My range can only be determined by what efforts enacted,
by examples of confidence proven after taking the first step.

Pillar

When we first met, I knew she would be my true pillar.
Nothing is greater than a solid base pillar.

So many mountains have been a burden on the journey alone.
Through thick and thin, hauling bags have been a supportive pillar.

For that reason, my comfort grew stronger.
I even remember a time when my shoulder was your pillar.

Together we could accomplish all that's important.
How less interesting and boring life can be without a pillar.

I can count the many times my kindness was taken for granted.
My day was topped when she said, "Thanks for being my pillar."

Round The Clock

I feel the hands on my back.
Yup! Forcing me forward.
Each step toward what's intended.

To stop!
Would be a shove to the ground.
So, I stride with weak eyelids.

I trust,
that whatever is meant I will gain.
I know, nothing comes easy.

To stop!
Would be an end toward future additions.
So, I continue with acceptance.

I admit my daily life is a verb.
There's no pause;
just the love of a legacy.

What Matters Most

*W*hat matters most to me is waking up
with the power to breathe a new day's life.

The existence has an abundance of love
waiting to be held, and waiting to be appreciated.

I address with a sincere "Good Morning",
in my mind knowing I'm anointed.

Protected under supreme filters
guaranteeing my deliverance into salvation.

My Definition

My definition is I'm truly living grateful.
So many things taken for granted, I understand it – so I pivot.

Opening heart, my better part. Classy! Tasteful!
Earning what I own, happy when alone – a peaceful space.

Culturally aware, anticipating bare challenges.
Unafraid to risk, for a greater embedded rich – self value.

Rebuilding a lost past, glad to enter fate.
Daily sacrifice, embracing the paid price – goal driven.

Unshaken or internally removed from how to.
Responsible for written thoughts, venting off – I express.

Supportive by nature, savior of low self-esteem.
Player on good teams, creator of big dreams – I stretch.

Lovers But Not Lovers

Music's sound waves massage ear drums before lustful romance.
Our thoughts pinching deeply within heart-felt nervous emotions.
Redden passion captures timeless moments, real words spoken.
Body delves into the summer climate, wiggle, jiggle, and dance.
Smooth grooves! Vibes holding tightly with both mighty calm hands.
Aroused by the erotic tingle inside blood veins flowing.
Adding to the culture spread wide across, the country is growing.
Forward motion boundless freedom chose happy open.

Held in contempt owning purpose-driven selfish intent.
Living worldly, fleshy and yes! Real themes, big dreams expressed.
Subject matter revolves around inner-city brilliance.
There are higher powers believed to be enmeshed far left.
But the passion is fire burning desire true love incense.
From a fondness for sounds, tones inhaled! Exhaled! Strong breath.

Lyrics
Bonus Section

Shine Beyond

The revelation revealed / and made / Hip Hop a part of me /
Before it grew up / and expanded its artistry /
We met up at a point in my life / it was the perfect time /
In the beginning / with break beats / and authentic rhymes /
Feeding the passion / addicted to a crowd reaction /
Punchline delivery / forcing heads to lean backwards / (pause)
Adrenaline rush / telling me / now or never /
Practicing my flow / then my skills started getting better /
My conscious / talking to me / like a mentor /
Debates / spark up inner conflict / flaming my temper /
Coaching my position / and challenging my potential /
Trying to play me out / like stupid questions / at a interview /
Heatwaves / blaze and burn / a bunch of blue flames /
As a rookie / was out of control / and untamed /
Words painting pictures / vividly like intuition /
Just to bring balance / in the center of the mechanism /

Season

*E*arly morning / full of rest / now I'm feeling fresh
woke with a lighter chest / stronger now I'm at my best /
nevertheless / stay focused / on making progress /
I calculated every step / so I can live without regret /
the picture clearer now / that's why I got a bigger smile /
standing on a firmer ground / you rolling / then hold me down /
swagger a better style / work hard / so Gouda pile /
I did it / as a bastard child / even with no-one around /
hungry as starving pits / locked behind a metal fence /
opportunity intense / I took it / to represent /
all the core elements / I'm definite / a better fix /
topic at the top of lists / talk coming out of lips /
driven by ambition / heart beating / like hot pistons /
I'm what the block been missing / written for the life I'm living /
I got a brighter vision / that furnace / the go in getting /
ready for the new beginning / took a loss / but now I'm winning /

Theory of Man

Aside from many different distractions /
that triggers an off balance /
nowhere to run / facing it all how it comes /
yet and still / missing the point of the process / the power build /
held to be accountable / versus doing the opposite /
testing if I'm a savage / or consciously using common sense /
it's nothing harder / than forces causing the shortage /
Interrupting the gravity / pulling from moving forward /
I see it now / all them gray clouds / filled with lessons /
growing from a boy to man / right or wrong direction /
seeking out a better life / living under the sun /
waiting for opportunities / hoping to be the one /
this equation / is a matter of strong mental ability /
trusting that it attract / everything that will keep it real with me /
so I center and pivot / focused / while pushing the limit /
making the best use of time / adding each second on minutes /

Theme

*I*n the line of action / these Gilligan Island's / hungry for captains /
Game tight / as air force one's / for better traction /
The lights flashing / pie cut me a bigger fraction /
Flow like currency / in casinos / that keep them gambling /
My ball bouncing / grind units / by the thousand /
Before the millions / turn easy / as water fountains /
Sixteen ounces of juice / and still counting /
Plus 48 more / just to equal a half gallon /
Ready to rock / more domes / than any stone thrown /
Them haters / leave them leaking out puddles / colored maroon /
5' 9" /and weighing a buck fifty-five /
That's no jive / even if I'm signed with Clive / ...

Tribute

(Dedicated to Mothers, Wives and Women)

$\mathcal{T}$he respect for a lady / is more than / just kind words
something special / real men / in this world deserve
I'm talking about / down to earth / with a sharp mind
always come through / for another / right at the perfect time
good spirit / compliments / how you carry it
always find a way / to make it through / them tough challenges
I can see it in your eyes / solid to the core
that grown woman / mentality / far above immature
the reason / I'm living / and walking on earth
made the final decision / to bring life / and give birth
you all about / the real / when it go down
tell it like it is / if you didn't / now, you know now
understand the struggles of man / lost / with no plans
fall to ground / you there extending / a helping hand
you more / than just / the average type of person
medicine / to the pains / I feel when I'm hurting

Momentum

I tightened my game / focused / steady aim /
sweating from the flame of fire / pumping inside my veins /
I got a hunger pain / nibbling on my stomach lining /
I'm the new Horizon / shining / like a bunch of diamonds /
climbing up mountains / Just to stand on the apex /
the feeling is good / like living life free / with no debt /
I always go left / that's how a man do /
controlling the ball / like a point guard / nice with handles /
flow animal / from the wilderness / called a beast /
butcher in the shop / that chop bones / and cut meat /
loss sleep / my grind strong / the whole week /
humble as a sheep / ready to bite / with sharp teeth /
low-key / and I never been the flashy type /
cooler than some faucet water / mixed in a glass of ice /
my calling / keep the street team balling /
7 days a week / starting early in the morning /

Quality Type

*I*t's the feeling that I get / next to your presence /
what's that fresh scent? /
Smelling good / like you should / there go the light-switch /
Turned on by your God gifts / can make a man feel nauseous /
That's why I'm so cautious /
So each effect / can identify what the cause is /
and your flaws is limited /
I bet you keep a lot of dudes / fumbling over sentences /
More than less / continuous / stare got a intimate trance /
In conflict with the thought of chance /
Pretty feet and small hands / metaphoric if you was sneakers /
Not bo bo's / a name brand /
I'm not the same as any Ex / or platonic friend /
And won't complain or stress / if you want the next man /
More power to the better / because I keep open my options /
In directions that's more interested /
settled for second and third best /
As an adolescent / since I've matured /
I deserve respect from the top selective /
Include the beauty of conscious / not just outer appearance /
Personality / conversation / and other bearings /
Let it be known up front / what my intentions are /
And when the time is appropriate / go a step farther /

Premeditated Seeds

*I*f I have a daughter / I plan to name her essence /
that be the best blessing / of all my creations /
here's your invitation — Boo! /you ready for the making /
the mood is just right / and I'm tired of just waiting /
twenty whole years / I had a vision of this moment /
before you / I couldn't never find a good woman /
to stay true / and feel comfortable / Cause what you do /
she gone do too / along with other things / that she might do /
my young star, moon, and earth / I'm there at birth /
and every single year / you grow into your woman's worth /
I'm a teach you / what you need to know / to overcome the worst /
and how to deal with the pain / if your feelings get hurt /
how I provide for you / is Royal (real) /
your mom says your spoiled /
that's only cause you act like me / and stay loyal /
my point of view of it all / I want the best for you /
that's why I'm next to you / and buy the best for you /
don't ever let a man / raise his hand to do you harm /
don't never think he love you / if he choose to do you wrong /
if he love you / he will show and embrace you in his arms /
similar to how I do / cause you a very / special charm /
now a days / some women / seem to be the breadwinner /
want to know what we doing / Even cook a nice dinner /
quick to bat / stepping up / a real hard hitter /
when support get delivered / a real go getter /
by any means / don't ever think you less than a queen /
I'm telling you — YOU BEAUTIFUL / born to be free /
learn a lesson from me / a few words from a king /
so you always think big / and pursue any dream /

Through the Experience

T he greatest joy / was the birth of Troy /
Through the experience / grown into a man from boy /
Cool different / Born with an intelligent mind /
Hard worker / now a days / something hard to find /
For some reason / when I reminisce / everything pause /
Replaying the scenes / when I'm right or wrong /
Appreciate how my family / always got my back /
Going through the ups and downs / of a cause and effect /
My Grandmother / was the first friend / that I ever had /
Moms played both roles / until she met my step dad /
My real dad / is a unknown source /
It's all good / we united through a spiritual force /
However, with all the differences / we still stay connected /
Know and understand / elders always get respected /
Walking on a thin line / tempted by temptations /
Abducted by superficial / instant gratification /

Safe

Hooking to better things in the lab cooking up meals /
the skills been imbedded / thorough since I was sperm /
my firm pitch / click with a measure that's hard earned /
now turn every page / I laid and feel stressed /
mad cause you know I get wreck it all reflect /
best inside the mirror / rep'n this new era /
wanted some shell tops /after watching tougher than leather /
better than alright / I came and still remain /
I never go away / I'm like jeans with grass stains /
strange to the ear that started a year ago /
my flow been running / how snot do nostrils /
my fossils get studied still inside the flesh /
my genes a rare set / foreseen before death / ...

Champion

No deal breaker / when we form a bond / tight as a know
The way I'm treated / will explain / the space I have in your heart
Your friends never come between / what we make it to be
Our mind power / strong enough / we think similar things
Gossip is not tolerate / conversation mature
Communicate clear and accurate / Without getting bored
By your side doing right / never rush to judge
Showing you / my definition / what it means to be loved
An attraction to the parts of you / my eyes can't witness
Inner core / is a display of an adorable image
One by one / every bad habit slowly diminish
The motivation that I'm feeling / keep me going the distance
My position / is shoe size / nobody else fit
A good man matching your standards / when you know what that is
We both aligned / through the soul / it's a natural vibe
So what we have is an investment / that is built over time.

```
E F A S E M G O D P F B E
Z U V W D O T V I R L T K
R B N D A M W K P E R Q L
T O U P R E D L S M P O J
H O S L E N O K C E S H I
R C E T P T K E I D N L U
O I H R E U V Q M I A B X
U A T K D M S D K T M Q S
G L R O L C T I C A F K R
H C E T P O K E L T O J D
T L D F Z D M X T E Y Z N
H I N K I E Q E S D R W O
E M U O H I Z C T S O H Y
E A R T L D S I K E E G E
X X I R F E P N E E H E B
P C D I X T O A O D T B E
E T H B D F P G C S P Q N
R W K U P I T R E C A N I
I X B T C G E O F F R E H
E R D E E F S X G D O P S
N Q K Z W S B N D L Q I W
C Z C H A M P I O N A L E
E G W M J A T U D G V S R
```

*W*ord Search: Find the *song titles* from the Lyrics section.

- *Shine Beyond*

- *Season*

- *Theory of Man*

- *Theme*

- *Tribute*

- *Momentum*

- *Quality Type*

- *Premeditated Seeds*

- *Through the Experience*

- *Safe*

- *Champion*

Acknowledgements

This book is to present a present voice of the many poets talking to us through poetry previous decades and centuries ago.

Thanks to all family and friends
Thanks to children and adults
Thanks to women and men
Thanks to other writers and poets
Thanks to all musicians and artist of all genres
Thanks to middle, high school, and college/university students
Thanks to the National Institutes of Health
Thanks to all bookstores and libraries
Thanks to professors and educators
Thanks to the Military (all branches)
Thanks to those incarcerated
Thanks to all countries that enjoy and respect poetry & literature
Thanks to editors
Thanks to Hiram Sims & the Community Literature Initiative family
Thanks to Sims Library of Poetry
Thanks to my 1st Semester Instructors:
    Valarie Niles, Camari Carter-Williams, Margaret Garcia
Thanks to my 2nd Semester Instructors:
    Margaret Garcia, Annalicia Agular
Thanks to both CLI Season 9 & 10 class students
Thanks to all my CLI Alumni Cohorts
Thanks to the hardworking CLI book production team
Thanks to Cathey Conte, who assisted with the first book cover design
Thanks to Thomas King for marketing and promotions assistance
Thanks to those who supported my poetry collection *Social Climax*

Special thanks go out to everyone who extended a hand

About the Author

A native of Trenton, New Jersey, Troy R. Legette is a writer, poet, author, and actor. He currently lives in the Central Florida area, working as a barber and an accountant. In addition, he's earned his Master's Degree in Accounting at University of Phoenix and is pursuing a Film & Media Degree at Arizona State University.

He blazes trails with his poetic parallelism of self-empowering speeches, education, nonfiction, and inspiration. He hopes his writing uplifts readers, helping heal their wounds and provide awareness based on his real-life experiences.

Legette self-published his first book of poetry, Social Climax, in 2015. It received good reviews online at Amazon and Barnes & Noble. He hopes to expand his audience with The Objective Scholar, his second poetry collection.

 His first book, *Social Climax,* was a landmark as an author

 His first professional music video was a song titled "Gifted"

 His second professional music video was a song titled "Shine Beyond Remix"

Website/Blog: www.troylegette.com

Instagram / Facebook / Twitter (X) / LinkedIn: @troyrlegette